Martin Luther King, Jr. Memorial

by Stephanie Fitzgerald

Content Consultant

Nanci R. Vargus, Ed.D.
Professor Emeritus, University of Indianapolis

Reading Consultant

Jeanne M. Clidas, Ph.D.
Reading Specialist

Children's Press®
An Imprint of Scholastic Inc.

Library of Congress Cataloging-in-Publication Data
Names: Fitzgerald, Stephanie, author.
Title: Martin Luther King, Jr. Memorial/by Stephanie Fitzgerald.
Description: New York, NY: Children's Press, An Imprint of Scholastic Inc., 2019. |
Series: Rookie national parks | Includes bibliographical references and index.
Identifiers: LCCN 2018028378 |
ISBN 9780531133217 (library binding: alk. paper) | ISBN 9780531137246
(pbk.: alk. paper)
Subjects: LCSH: Martin Luther King, Jr., Memorial (Washington, D.C.)—Juvenile
literature. | Memorials—Washington (D.C.) —Juvenile literature.
Classification: LCC F203.4.M118 F58 2019 | DDC 975.3—dc2

Produced by Spooky Cheetah Press
Design: Ed LoPresti Graphic Design
Creative Direction: Judith E. Christ for Scholastic Inc.

Published in 2019 by Children's Press, an imprint of Scholastic Inc.

Printed in Heshan, China 62

SCHOLASTIC, CHILDREN'S PRESS, ROOKIE NATIONAL PARKS™, and
associated logos are trademarks and/or registered trademarks of Scholastic Inc.

1 2 3 4 5 6 7 8 9 10 R 28 27 26 25 24 23 22 21 20 19

Scholastic, Inc., 557 Broadway, New York, NY 10012.

Photos ©: cover: Mira Agron/Dreamstime; back cover: Steve Lagreca/Shutterstock; 1, 2:
Cleo Design/Shutterstock; 3: Sean Pavone/Shutterstock; 4-5: Brian Irwin/Dreamstime; 6:
DigitalGlobe/Getty Images; 8: Everett Collection; 11: AP Images; 12-13: Photo 12/UIG/Getty
Images; 13 inset: Moneta Sleet, Jr./Ebony Collection/AP Images; 14 inset: Joseph Louw/The
LIFE Images Collection/Getty Images; 14-15: Bettmann/Getty Images; 16: Jacquelyn Martin/
AP Images; 17: Liu Jin/AFP/Getty Images; 18-19: kropic1/Shutterstock; 20-21: Winston Tan/
Shutterstock; 21 inset: The Washington Post/Getty Images; 22-23: The Washington Post/Getty
Images; 24-25: U.S. National Park Service; 26 top left: Everett Collection; 26 top right: AP
Images; 26 bottom: Don Cravens/The LIFE Images Collection/Getty Images; 27 top: Bettmann/
Getty Images; 27 bottom left: Moneta Sleet, Jr./Ebony Collection/AP Images; 27 bottom right:
Sophie James/Shutterstock; 30: Hulton Archive/Getty Images; 31 top: Photo 12/UIG/Getty
Images; 31 center top: Moneta Sleet, Jr./Ebony Collection/AP Images; 31 center bottom:
Donald Uhrbrock/The LIFE Images Collection/Getty Images; 31 bottom: Don Cravens/The LIFE
Images Collection/Getty Images; 32: Mandel Ngan/AFP/Getty Images.

"Ranger Red Fox" by Bill Mayer for Scholastic

Maps by Jim McMahon/Mapman ®

Table of Contents

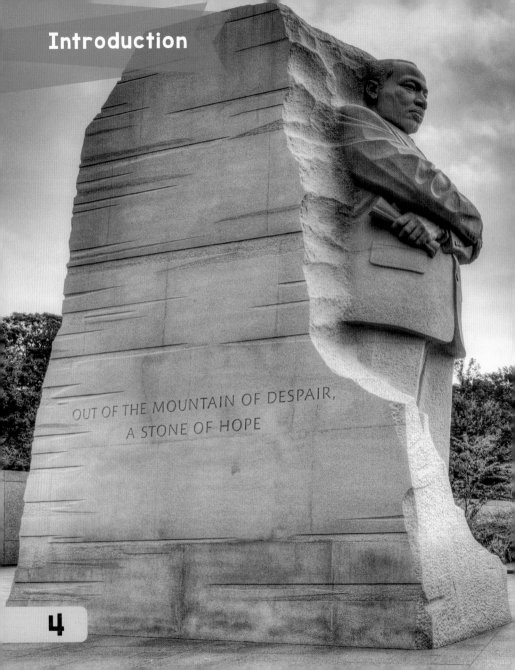

OUT OF THE MOUNTAIN OF DESPAIR,
A STONE OF HOPE

Welcome to the Martin Luther King, Jr. Memorial!

The Martin Luther King, Jr. Memorial is in Washington, D.C. It was created for **civil rights** leader Martin Luther King, Jr. He fought for justice and equality for African Americans.

I am Ranger Red Fox, your tour guide. Are you ready for an amazing adventure at the Martin Luther King, Jr. Memorial?

This is a portion of the National Mall.

Martin Luther King, Jr., is known as "MLK."

◄ ········ MLK Memorial

United States

Washington, D.C.→

National Mall

The memorial is part of the National Mall in Washington, D.C. It is the first monument on the mall to **honor** an African American!

The memorial has a cool address: 1964 Independence Avenue. The Civil Rights Act of 1964 was one of the most important civil rights laws in U.S. history. MLK played a big part in making that law happen.

Martin poses with his parents, grandmother, and siblings.

Martin Luther King, Jr.

Chapter 1

Meet Martin Luther King, Jr.

King was born in Atlanta, Georgia, in 1929. During that time, Georgia and other areas in the South had unfair laws. African American people were treated badly, simply because of the color of their skin. MLK fought his entire life to end this unfair treatment.

King was always a very good student. He finished college when he was just 19 years old. After that, he went back to school to become a **pastor**.

MLK wanted life to be fair for everyone. He used peaceful ways to bring about change. He gave speeches and led marches to **protest** unfair treatment.

King delivered his famous "I Have a Dream" speech at the March on Washington.

About 250,000 people heard King speak at the March on Washington for Jobs and Freedom in 1963.

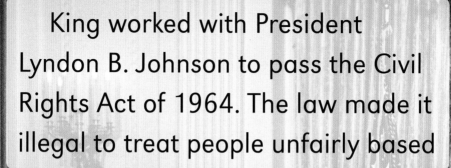

King worked with President Lyndon B. Johnson to pass the Civil Rights Act of 1964. The law made it illegal to treat people unfairly based

Martin Luther King, Jr.

President Johnson

The Civil Rights Act is signed into law.

12

on the color of their skin. That same year, King was awarded the Nobel Peace Prize for his work.

At the time, King was the youngest person ever to win the Nobel Peace Prize.

A lot of people, both black and white, joined MLK in his fight for justice. But some white people did not want to see him succeed. On April 4, 1968, James Earl Ray shot and killed MLK.

After his death, people looked for ways to honor Dr. King.

After the shooting, King's friends pointed to where the shots came from.

As many as 50,000 people joined King's funeral procession.

A scale model, or miniature version, of the winning design.

The scale model shows the many cherry trees around the MLK Memorial.

Chapter 2

A Dream Project

The Martin Luther King, Jr. National Memorial Project Foundation was created in 1996. The group chose a spot for a memorial to King. Then a competition was held to decide who would build it. The winning design was selected in 2000.

An artist named Master Lei Yixin was chosen to create the sculpture.

The Stone of Hope is 30 feet (9 meters) tall and made of 159 granite blocks.

Mountain of Despair

The design was inspired by a line from a famous MLK speech. He said: "With this faith we will be able to hew [carve] out of the mountain of despair

Stone of Hope

OUT OF THE MOUNTAIN OF DESPAIR,
A STONE OF HOPE

a stone of hope." Two large pieces of stone represent the Mountain of Despair. A carving of King is shown as the Stone of Hope.

Another important part of the memorial is the wall that runs behind the large sculptures. Fourteen of MLK's most famous quotes are engraved there.

The inscription wall is 450 feet (137 meters) long.

King used his words, not his fists, to fight for equality. He spoke of a better future. He worked to make his dream a reality.

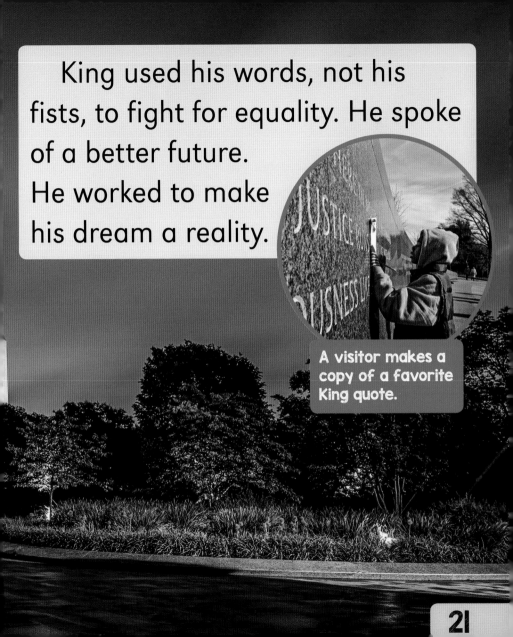

A visitor makes a copy of a favorite King quote.

More than
3 million people
visit the memorial
every year.

Chapter 3

The Memorial Today

The Martin Luther King, Jr. Memorial was officially dedicated on August 28, 2011. That was the 48th anniversary of the March on Washington for Jobs and Freedom. Every year in April, many people honor King's life and leadership by visiting the memorial on the same day that he died.

The Martin Luther King, Jr. Memorial was made to inspire people. All of its parts were carefully picked to show King's impact on the world. People visit to remember what MLK achieved—and to find hope for the future.

Read about some key moments in the life of Martin Luther King, Jr.

MLK leads
the Montgomery
Bus Boycott.

1929

1955

1963

MLK
is born.

King gives
his famous
"I Have a Dream"
speech at the
March on
Washington
for Jobs and
Freedom.

MLK is one of just four non-presidents to have a memorial on the National Mall.

King receives the Nobel Peace Prize.

The memorial opens.

| 1964 | 1968 | 2011 |

Martin Luther King, Jr. is killed.

Where Is Ranger Red Fox?

Oh no! Ranger Red Fox has lost his way on the National Mall. But you can help. Use the map and the clues below to find him.

1. Ranger Red Fox was reading the quotes on the wall at the MLK Memorial.

2. He started walking northwest. He saw a long pool of water in front of a large statue of President Abraham Lincoln.

3. Next, he walked north to visit the Vietnam Veterans Memorial.

4. Finally, he walked east along Constitution Avenue until he got to the newest museum on the National Mall.

Help! Can you find me?

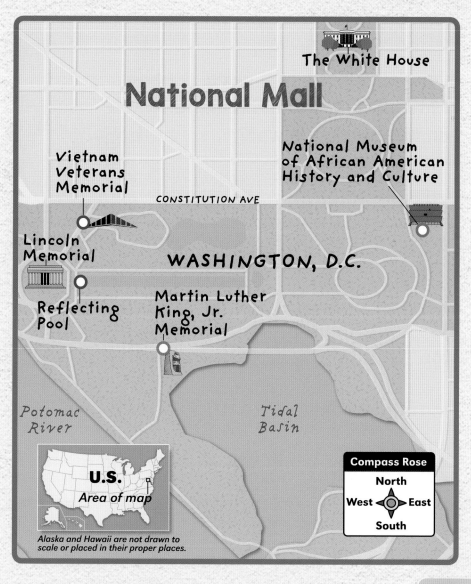

National Mall

The White House

National Museum of African American History and Culture

Vietnam Veterans Memorial

CONSTITUTION AVE

Lincoln Memorial

WASHINGTON, D.C.

Reflecting Pool

Martin Luther King, Jr. Memorial

Potomac River

Tidal Basin

U.S.
Area of map

Alaska and Hawaii are not drawn to scale or placed in their proper places.

Compass Rose

North

West ◆ East

South

Can you guess which word fills in each blank in this quote on the inscription wall?

King speaks at the March on Washington.

World   Equal   Person

"Make a career of humanity.

Commit yourself to the noble struggle

for _____(1)_____ rights. You will

make a greater _____(2)_____ of yourself,

a greater nation of your country, and a

finer _____(3)_____ to live in."

Answers: 1. equal; 2. person; 3. world

Glossary

civil rights (**siv**-uhl rites): freedom and equal treatment under the law

honor (**ah**-nur): to praise someone or give him or her an award

pastor (**pass**-tuhr): minister or priest in charge of a church or parish

protest (**proh**-test): a demonstration or statement against something

Index

Facts for Now

Visit this Scholastic Web site for more information on the Martin Luther King, Jr. Memorial:
www.factsfornow.scholastic.com
Enter the keywords **MLK Memorial**

About the Author

Stephanie Fitzgerald loves writing nonfiction for kids because it gives her the chance to learn more about some of her favorite subjects, such as the Civil Rights Movement and Dr. King.